Archie
and Archie

ARCHIE AND ARCHIE
A BODLEY HEAD BOOK 978 1 782 30005 2

Published in Great Britain by The Bodley Head,
an imprint of Random House Children's Publishers UK
A Random House Group Company

This edition published 2013

1 3 5 7 9 10 8 6 4 2

The Random House Group Limited supports the Forest Stewardship Council® (FSC®), the
leading international forest-certification organisation. Our books carrying the FSC label are
printed on FSC®-certified paper. FSC is the only forest-certification scheme supported by the
leading environmental organisations, including Greenpeace. Our paper procurement policy
can be found at www.randomhouse.co.uk/environment

MIX
Paper from
responsible sources
FSC
www.fsc.org
FSC® C016897

Typeset in 13/16.5pt Minion Regular by Falcon Oast Graphic Art Ltd.

RANDOM HOUSE CHILDREN'S PUBLISHERS UK
61–63 Uxbridge Road, London W5 5SA

www.**randomhousechildrens**.co.uk
www.**totallyrandombooks**.co.uk
www.**randomhouse**.co.uk

Addresses for companies within The Random House Group Limited can be found at:
www.randomhouse.co.uk/offices.htm

THE RANDOM HOUSE GROUP Limited Reg. No. 954009

A CIP catalogue record for this book is available from the British Library.

Printed and bound in Great Britain by
Clays Ltd, St Ives plc

Archie and Archie

Ruth Rendell

Illustrated by Madeleine Floyd

THE BODLEY HEAD

Meet the Characters

Archie Cat

Archie Dog

Pearl

Rosie and her puppies

Gracie

White Leg

Loki

The Animals at Home

Misty had five kittens, and when they were ten days old I went to see them. The golden kitten, Archie, was never very small; he was always big and strong. I chose him for his colour and his golden eyes, and his sister Pearl because she was pearl-grey, though she too had golden eyes. When they were ten weeks old I brought them home with me. They sat in a box in the back of the car and cried all the way. But when I let them out, they walked all over the house, getting to know everything.

The vet said they had to stay inside for four weeks. I didn't know then how often Archie would get lost in the years to come. Pearl only got lost once. She was the good quiet cat; Archie was the naughty one, and a fighter. He squealed a lot, and mewed and howled too.

He began to grow into a fine animal, the colour of a lion, with the most beautiful stripy tail – orange and cream – that you ever will see. When the kittens were allowed out, they didn't go

beyond
the garden at
first. But they
soon became braver,
and then they got lost.

I looked for them everywhere. I called on all my neighbours to ask if they had seen Archie or Pearl. No one had. It began to get dark, and then, at the top of the scaffolding around a big building, a bright light came on. I looked up towards it, and there on the scaffolding, as high as they could get, were Archie and Pearl. The light dazzled them and they dashed back down into the garden and through their cat flap.

One of the houses I called at was the one where Archie the dog came to live, years and years later. Like Pearl, he is quiet and good. Everyone he meets on his walks wants to stroke and pat him. Archie the dog likes that: he is very friendly. He even likes Archie the cat. When I go out into the garden to call my Archie – "Archie, Archie, come in now!" –

Archie the dog comes running out of his house because he thinks I am calling him. He is a very pretty dog – a King Charles spaniel. His fur is black and white but his neck and eyebrows are tan-coloured. He has dark eyes and silky ears. Every day my Archie goes down the garden, over the wall into next door's, then over another wall into Archie the dog's garden. There he sits on top of a tall pillar. When Archie the dog sees him, he comes out of his house and stands under the pillar, looking up at my Archie and barking. They stare at each other but they aren't cross.

Sometimes my Archie carries on into the churchyard. On the other side of the wall are trees and bushes and wild places where grey squirrels and foxes live – along with tiny animals like mice and shrews.

It is quiet and shady and not much like London. What does Archie the cat do in there? I think he goes hunting. I know he finds a pond – because once he fell into it, looking for frogs and fish. I thought I had lost him, and when he came back he looked quite unlike my Archie. He was black with mud and covered in sticky, smelly pondweed. It took him a whole hour to lick off the mud until he was clean and fresh again.

Archie's Sister Pearl

So where was my little pearl-grey Pearl? I haven't said much about her for a sad reason. She is dead. She lived with Archie and me for a long time, but one warm summer's day she was out lying in the sun and became very ill. I took her to the vet, who sent her to the cat and dog hospital, where they found that she had cancer. She had an operation. All the people at the hospital were very kind and caring. Though I went to visit her, poor Pearl missed her home. After a second operation she died.

I was very sad without her. Was Archie sad? I think he must have been because he looked all over the house for her – upstairs and downstairs, in all the rooms, under the tables and chairs. Then he looked around the garden and in other people's gardens. And then he seemed to forget, and he was his old happy self again.

All Archie and I now have of Pearl is a photo in a silver frame.

The Horses

In my living room there is a big table close by the window. Archie and Pearl used to sit on the table and look down at the animals in the street. Now only Archie sits there. He can see Archie the dog going out for his morning walk and then his midday walk.

The police take their horses out along the street on the other side of the canal.

Sometimes there are as many as twenty horses trotting past. It doesn't happen often, but when it does and Archie is on the table to see it, he gets very excited. He sits completely still – except for his tail, which swings from side to side. His eyes grow very large and glow like lamps, and as the horses pass by, their hooves going *clop-clop-clop*, he makes a little sound – a squeak and then another squeak. I think he would like the horses to go by every day so that he could watch them and wave his tail and squeak.

Other Cats and Dogs

Another cat lives next door to Archie the dog. Her name is Gracie. She has a very pretty face, and is small and neat; her fur is the colour of a Brazil nut, but soft and sleek. She moves very fast, and when she meets a cat or dog she doesn't like, she hisses. She opens her mouth wide and makes a noise like this: *Hisssshh!*

My Archie and Gracie don't like each

other at all. Once I saw Archie grab her by the leg and tip her into a flower bed. Now she hates him, and when she can she smacks him and scratches his face. Archie and Gracie walk round and round and round each other in circles, getting very cross.

When they stop circling each other, they have a little fight and make loud noises – wails and howls and squeals. Then they run home. Gracie jumps over the wall into her garden. Archie climbs over the shed

and slides back into my garden. Beside the shed is a big bush that I call Archie's bush. He hides inside it when he doesn't want to be found.

When he was a kitten Archie the cat used to go out into the street, but now he never does. He doesn't like the cars and he doesn't like the canal. He knows that dogs live on some of the boats there. One of them is called Rosie. She is black all over and has a very sweet nature. There is another boat dog who is her friend. He too is black, his name is Nero and he barks a lot from his boat. Now Rosie has had five puppies. Nero is their father. I haven't seen them yet – they are still very little – and nor has Archie. They are sure to be coal-black. I wonder how these puppies will like living on a boat. One of them will stay there with Rosie. All the others are going to new homes when they are old enough.

Another canal dog is black and white, and the same breed of spaniel as Archie the dog. Her name is Tess. There is also a cat who lives on a boat: his name is just Cat, so I call him the Boat Cat. He is small and sleek, with a completely black coat, and he wears a smart red collar with a medal hanging from it. He has a cat flap that he can pop in and out of so he can come ashore. I like to see him poke his

head out, then his furry body and his tail. Because he is a cat and very wary and careful, he looks right and left and across the canal, and then jumps across the few inches of water that lie between the boat deck and the canal bank. He is often in my front garden: he opens his mouth wide to mew at me, and I know he wants to come into my house. But that can never be. If I let the Boat Cat in, Archie would know at once and come roaring out to drive him away. When he had done that he would come to me to be stroked and petted. But fighting the Boat Cat is not allowed.

A cat called Loki used to live in Gracie's house. He was a Bengal cat, stripy like a tiger. He and Archie used to fight all the time. They punched and scratched each other, and rolled over and over, screaming and howling, and bit pieces out of each other's ears. Almost every week they had to go to the vet to have their wounds treated. And then one day Loki moved away with his family. He was very good to look at and fond of his people, but I was glad to see him go so that the fighting would stop. Now Archie fights with Gracie, but their fights are not so bad and no one gets hurt.

Our houses face the canal and are all joined together in a long block. Along this runs a balcony that you can get on to by going out of a bedroom window. At first Archie longed to get out of my bedroom window and walk along the balcony all the way up to the church, and then to where the flats begin. He also liked to get up on his hind legs and look through windows at people going to bed, but this was rude so I had to stop him. This made him sad. He sat by the closed window and cried softly, still hoping to get into someone else's house. It wasn't enough for him to go hunting in the church grounds or sit on the pillar in Archie the dog's garden or have a little fight with Gracie.

One day he would get into someone else's house and find out what was inside. A window would be left open, and he would jump inside and explore. But would he be able to get out again?

A Day in the Life of Archie the Dog

Archie is a very happy dog. You can see he is happy – he is always cheerful and pleased with life. He is lucky because his people take him out for four walks every day. The first walk is at seven-thirty in the morning. When he comes back he has his breakfast – biscuits and cereal and milk. He has another walk at midday, one in the evening and one at night, and when he is

out he often sees Rosie on her boat, or on
the canal path: he pushes his nose against
the rail and she brings hers up to touch it.
Will Rosie let him meet her puppies when

they come up on deck? We shall see.

Archie also meets Tess. Like him, she goes for lots of walks. She and Archie look a lot like each other. Both have long ears and long tails like feathers. Archie is black and white but also has tan markings, while Tess is just black and white. Archie's ears are like a girl's hair: black and silky and all waves and curls.

For his dinner Archie has dog food mixed with cooked meat. He always eats everything up and clears his plate. At night he sleeps upstairs with his people. He likes having a bath. When he is taken to the bathroom he knows what will happen so he jumps into the bathtub, all ready for his shampoo and shower.

When his owners go away, they don't send Archie to kennels; instead, a lady and her son come to take care of him in his own house. It is the same for Archie the cat. Dogs and cats are very fond of their homes and like to stay there.

White Leg and Archie

There is a black cat with one white leg (I don't know his name, but I call him White Leg) who lives on this side of the canal, further up the street near the main road – though he likes to cross the canal and explore the other side. He is a wise cat and keeps away from the busy road with all the cars and trucks, so to get to the other side he slips quietly through the café on

the bridge. The people who go to the café all recognize White Leg when he passes along the terrace, but he takes no notice of any of them.

At about nine o'clock I shut the cat flap for the night – though if I am out for the evening, Archie stays out in the garden until he sees the light go on. Then he comes in through the flap. But he likes it best if I open the garden door for him, because then I stroke him and tell him he is a good cat. Up in my bedroom I brush him with a rubber brush to keep his coat nice. Archie loves being brushed. Then he goes downstairs, but comes back to me at dawn and lies on the bed beside me, very close and warm. He always comes back – except for the night he didn't.

The Blue Collar with Diamonds

Archie the cat has a bar code planted in his back which a vet or the police can read if someone finds him. He has had collars, but he won't wear them. He isn't like the Boat Cat, who seems proud to wear his red collar with the medal. Archie has had seven collars – one black, two green, one brown, one silver, one pink and a fine dark blue one with diamonds on it. They weren't real

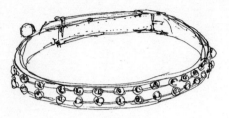 diamonds but they looked like diamonds. He pulled each one of those collars off and lost them. He must have left them lying in other people's gardens because two of them were brought back to me. But no one brought back the blue one with diamonds. It may still be lying out there under a bush in the church grounds. Or maybe someone found it and put it on their own cat.

It was no use putting the collars on him again; he would only lose them. Archie the cat hates collars. So he wasn't wearing one when he went missing.

Archie the Dog at Home

Archie the dog also has a smart collar with diamonds – or what look like diamonds. It is made of black leather and is very chic. Sometimes he sits on the couch and watches TV. If he sees a picture of a real animal – a dog or cat or rabbit, or even a lion – he seems to know it is real and barks at it. But when it's a cartoon animal like Tom or Jerry or Gromit, he understands

that it's not real and takes no notice of it.
He likes to sit on his special cushion on the
couch while he watches TV.

When he goes out with his owners, he
is very good in the car, and in shops he
sits down quietly. His people can take
him into restaurants and he doesn't ask
for food but just settles down beside their
table. His owner takes him with her to the
hairdresser's. Archie the dog sits in the

window and watches the people go by. When a clean, cheerful person passes by he wags his tail, but when the passer-by looks fierce or cross or dirty he barks.

Does he think he is looking after his owner? Does he see himself as a guard dog? Once, when he was younger, he was out for a walk in the park with his owner. There was a bull terrier running about off the lead. When it saw Archie walking along beside his owner, it flew at him and attacked him. Poor Archie screamed. His owner picked him up and hugged him tightly. The owner of the bull terrier said that her dog was always good and quiet, but Archie's owner said that if she ever saw the bull terrier in the park again without his lead, she would call the police.

Now if Archie ever sees a bull terrier,

he gets angry and tries to attack it. He remembers the dog in the park. Dogs and cats do remember things that have upset them – as Archie the cat would show me.

When Archie the Cat Was Missing

When Archie was younger he got lost. On summer evenings he used to go out into the garden and not come back for hours. I went to bed because I knew that he would come back in the night and jump (very quietly and softly) onto my bed. Then one night he didn't come back. I went out into the garden and called him: "Archie, Archie, come in now. Time to come in." But there was no sign of him.

The cat flap was open so he could come in when he liked. The morning came but there was no sign of Archie. It was a fine warm summer's day, and I went to the end of the garden and called to him over the wall. Unfortunately I had to go out. All the time I was away I thought about him and where he might be, though when I got back I was sure I would find him asleep on a chair. But he wasn't there. I was very worried. I called on all my neighbours and asked if anyone had seen Archie. But no one had. I phoned vets and the police to find if out whether he had been picked up. No one had seen him.

He didn't come back the next day, or the next. I stuck photos of him up on posts and trees in the street with his name and

LOST CAT

Archie

Please help us find our cat. If you see him please ring 0207 131 0264

my phone number on them.

But no one found him. I was lonely without him. I missed him a lot and I was worried. I tried to think where he might be. Shut in a shed or a garage? Had he got inside a car and been driven away?

I'd forgotten about the balcony and Archie looking in at the windows and crying. But later on I tried to get inside Archie's mind and work out where he might be. This is what I thought: Off he went that summer evening – over the wall, over the next wall into Archie the dog's garden, and on and on. It was warm, the sun was hot and it was nice to lie in the sunshine and sleep. When he woke up he walked a little further, hunted for a while but caught nothing. Then it was night time, it was dark: time to go home. But instead of going home, he walked on until he came to a very high wall. He wanted to know what was on the other side – he had never been there before – so he leaped up on top of it. Beyond was the garden of the flats. Archie jumped down onto the grass.

It was so late that the flats were all dark, but the moon was shining and there were a few bright stars. There was an open window in one of the ground-floor flats. That was a piece of luck, for now he could go in and at last see what it was like in someone else's home. In he went, and found himself in a room very like the ones he knew – though it smelled very different. He walked through room after room. Cats can see in the dark, and in one room he saw two people in bed, asleep. He was tired now, so he crept into a corner, curled up on the soft carpet and went to sleep.

In the night he heard people moving about; a window closed, and then a door. It was getting light. He stood up, stretched and looked around. Time to go home. Slowly he strolled back to the window he had come through the night before, but it was no longer open. He was shut in.

He padded around the whole flat, looking for a way out. In the bathroom the tap was dripping, making a small puddle

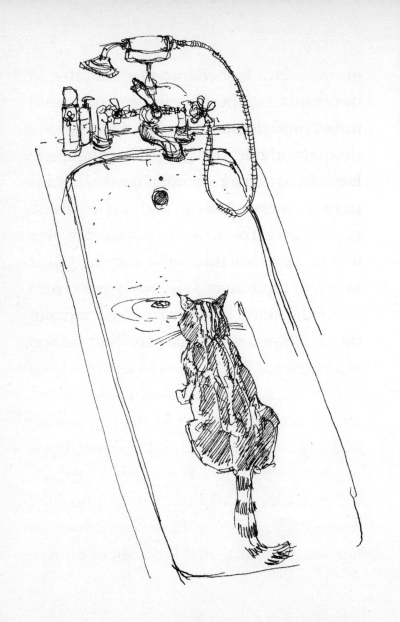

of water. He climbed into the bathtub and drank some. The people who had been in bed would come back, he thought. He slept again, but when he woke the people hadn't come back. A night passed, a day passed, then another night. He drank more water from the dripping tap. He was hungry, but there was nothing to eat in any of the rooms. It was very warm and stuffy. The days passed – five, six, seven of them. He was shut inside the flat; he was in prison.

Escape

On the eighth day he woke up to hear the front door open and close and big heavy bags being dropped on the floor. He stayed where he was. Footsteps crossed the floor and he heard the window being pushed up. It was too soon to go. He must wait. After a while he got up, stretched and crept to the door of the bedroom. The bags were open on the floor, still full of clothes. The two people were in bed, asleep. Archie wasted no time. Within a minute he was out of that window; he was free.

Over the high wall, into the church grounds, over more walls and more gardens, across Archie the dog's garden, and the next one, and into his own. He pushed open the cat flap and slipped inside. The person he shared his home with was sitting at the table eating breakfast. When she saw him she cried out, "Oh, Archie, Archie, it's you!" She picked him up and hugged and kissed him, but Archie struggled because he was hungry. She opened a can of meat and filled his plate. When he had eaten he curled up in an armchair and went to sleep for a long, long time.

The Haunted Stairs

That is what I think happened: the people who lived in the flat closed the window and went away on holiday. When they came back after a week, it was so hot in the flat that the first thing they did was open the window again. They were tired after a long flight and went to sleep. They never saw Archie.

Later on a funny thing happened. I

work at the top of the house and Archie always used to come up there with me. He padded into my room and jumped onto the desk. From there he could gaze out of the window, just as he could from the table below, but when he was up so much higher he could look into the branches of the plane tree, and at the magpies' nest there. The birds sit on their eggs, and later on they feed their chicks. Archie used to gnash his teeth at them and wave his tail.

But now he no longer comes up. He comes up as far as my bedroom, and there he stops. There are twelve more stairs up to my work room and the window and the plane tree and the magpies' nest. Archie sits on the bottom stair and looks up, and his eyes go very big and round, and he sees something I can't see because he

starts to howl. He howls and howls. If you have never heard a cat howl, you don't know what a horrid sound it is. I sit next to him on the bottom stair and tell him it is all right, there is nothing there, and I stroke him and hug him. At last he stops, but he won't come up those twelve stairs. He runs down to the living room and out through the cat flap to his bush. He has been up those stairs just twice since he disappeared for that week. I sat on each one of the twelve steps and called him and stroked him as he slowly climbed them, one after another. But when he was up there he wouldn't stay. He was too afraid of something that he could see or feel and I couldn't.

Like Archie the dog, he remembers.

I think that there is something in those rooms at the top that reminds him of his prison. It smells like the flat, or has similar furniture – the computer, the printer, the desk. He is afraid that if he goes into that room he will be shut in again, with nothing to eat, and no one to let him out. I don't think he will ever go up there again: he will never forget what happened when he was shut in.

The Second Time in Prison

This happened only a few months ago, but it was much worse than Archie's first disappearance. *That* time he was gone for eight days. This time he was missing for twelve. I had given him up for lost.

He went out, as he usually did, at about six in the evening. I waited for him, but he didn't appear. He didn't come back all night. We posted photos of him with my phone number on the trees down the street again. We told the local vets, we searched the big school nearby, and the church and the church garden. Kind people phoned and called to say they had spotted Archie, but it was another cat they had seen.

The days went by. I always knew Archie would come home when he could. If he could escape from the prison he was in this time, he would come back because he loves his home. I was very sad without him. I didn't eat or sleep much. Twelve days after Archie went missing I was standing in my bedroom looking out of the window and thinking that I would never see him again; it was so long, I assumed he must be dead. And then I heard loud crying from downstairs. At first I thought, *It can't be Archie*. But it *was*. He had come in through his cat flap and was waiting for his supper.

I filled his dish with food and he ate it up very fast. He drank some water, and then he walked over to the foot of the stairs, waiting for me to go up with him. He had got very thin. All the bones in his spine stuck out like knobs. We went upstairs and we went to bed. That night, at last, I slept, cuddling Archie.

So where had he been? We found out. Only four houses away, in a ground-floor flat. The people who live there had gone away and taken their cats with them. But they had left their cat flap so that a cat could go in but the cat couldn't get out again. That cat was Archie. The long time in prison had begun: twelve days of it. Finally a lady in another flat heard poor Archie crying. She got hold of a key, went in, opened the cat flap and let Archie out. It was evening by then, and dark. But cats like the dark, and once he was free Archie came straight home – across the neighbouring gardens, over the walls, into his own garden and at last through his cat flap.

While he was away Gracie visited my garden every day and looked in at the window. When Archie came back and was sitting beside me on the sofa, she came and looked in at us. Archie saw her, let out a yell, and rushed out to chase her down the garden. He hasn't changed and nor has she. They had one of their fights, making a big noise about it. Archie came back into the house. Cats can't smile, but he looked as if he was trying to. He was saying to himself, *I am home and everything is back to normal.*

Will he ever get lost again? I hope not, but I fear so. Because if a cat finds an open door, a window or a cat flap, he always wants to know what is inside. Cats are made that way and won't change.